What, Exactly, Is

Business
Development?

What, Exactly, Is

Business Development?

A Primer on Getting Deals Done

SCOTT POLLACK

firneo

What, Exactly, Is Business Development? A Primer on Getting Deals Done
by Scott Pollack

ISBN: 978-1-5217-7050-4

firneo.com

Contents

What Is Business Development?

My name is Scott Pollack, and for the past 15 years, I've worked in business development. What do I even mean when I say that? What exactly is business development? ... That's what this book is all about.

This book is not just business development for startups, or business development for large companies. It's about business development for everyone. This book is all about explaining how business development is done at companies of all sizes, so that you can apply that understanding to your company.

I've been in your shoes before. I've been in the trenches at startups, I've run my own company, and I've done deals for startups like WeWork and big companies like American Express. I know what it's like to be overwhelmed with ideas for how you can develop your business. How do you actually generate sales? How do you create partnerships? How do you build relationships that will create long-term opportunities?

In addition to working in business development, I've also taught it to thousands of students around the country at corporate workshops, startup accelerators, and top business schools like Harvard, Wharton, Babson, and NYU. I've taught thousands of students about business development, and given them the tools to build a career in business development. Using the same concepts that are in this book, I've shown them how to pursue the right growth opportunities that will help them scale their companies.

This book will help demystify and clarify the inner workings of business development. My goal is to give you a system for thinking about business development, helping to put your career on the right track.

To really dig deeply into this topic, it's important that we start by being on the same page. We're going to define what business development is, why it matters, and how it works. We're also going to talk about the skills that are necessary for business development people to do a good job. And we're also going to talk about what the day job of business development actually is — the core job functions — at companies of all sizes.

Next, we're going to talk about the big-picture strategies of business development. What are the ways that you can be thinking about growth opportunities strategically, helping to ensure that you're always focusing on the right ones?

Finally, we're going to talk about the tactics of business development. What are the actual steps that you need to take to get in the door? What actions do you need to take to land partnership deals and win sales, regardless of the size of your company?

CHAPTER 1

Defining Business Development

How do you define business development? Maybe you think of it in terms of sales, partnerships, or new lines of business. Perhaps you see it in terms of growth, or new revenue streams.

Here's the thing: All of those sound correct. Depending on the context, any of them could be an accurate description of a specific business development job. There is no single, universally accepted definition. In fact, if you look in almost any dictionary for the term "business development," it is literally undefined.

That's the challenge with business development. There are many disparate ways to talk about the idea of business development, but no single, clearly defined definition that we can all agree on. Unless we're all on the same page on what business development is, how can we have a serious discussion about how to do it better?

To help me gain a better understanding of what business development really is, I've spent thousands of hours talking with business experts, entrepreneurs, CEOs and presidents of Fortune 500 firms, as well as people on the front lines of startups and companies of all sizes. Each conversation gave me a new perspective, helping me to consolidate those disparate views into a single definition that reconciles all those different ways of thinking about the term.

Here it is:

> *Business Development is creating*
> *long-term value for an organization*
> *from customers, markets,*
> *and relationships.*

Let's take a look at that definition in more detail.

The concept of value is a good place to start. Business development is all about creating opportunities to pursue value. What exactly is value, and how can we start to think about the value of opportunities?

What Is Value?

Value is inherently subjective. Something that is highly valuable to one person — like rare stamps or vintage LPs — might not be valuable at all to someone else. To a collector, a rare book might be worth thousands, while to another it's just some old relic gathering dust on a shelf.

Value also isn't static. What's valuable to me today might not be valuable to me tomorrow. People will trample each other to buy the last remaining popular kids' toy on Christmas Eve, even if they know that the shelves will be stocked with them a week after New Year's Eve. Before we can discuss the role that value plays in business development, we need to define the concept of value in a new way.

Think about the things that you personally value. You may value money, but chances are that you place an even greater value on the things that money allows you to do. Perhaps you value time with your family and friends. You may value the lifestyle you've created for yourself, the career you've built, the financial security you've worked for, or even your health.

Which of these represent "real" value? All of them. Value means something different to everyone.

The same is true for businesses. While every company wants to make money, each one has a unique perspective on what they value, and money may only be one of those things. Each business will see value in different terms. When you're thinking about opportunities from a business development standpoint, it's important to remember that every opportunity might create a different type of value.

Value wears many different hats, takes many shapes, and has many different faces. Let's take a look at some of the most important kinds of value for business development.

ECONOMIC VALUE

The most fundamental way that we think about value in the context of business is economic value. For instance, "Does it make me money?" Economic value is generally discussed in terms of revenue and profit.

It is completely fair to talk about the job of business development in terms of economic value. Things that generate profit and revenue are often great ways to generate long-term value for an organization. It's just as important to understand, however, that economic value is not the only form of value. There are other kinds of value that are just as important from an business development perspective.

BRAND VALUE

Brand value is the overall benefit of changing the perception of the company in the eyes of our partners, customers, and prospective customers. One of the most valuable things a company can have is a strong brand identity, yet relatively few people think of the brand itself as a form of value.

To illustrate this point, let's talk about one of the best-known brands on the planet: Coca-Cola. Every year, Coca-Cola spends billions of dollars on marketing and advertisements. The goal behind all that spending isn't just to get people to buy more cans of soda, it's also to get you to associate their brand with everything and everything so that you are always thinking about Coke.

Generating brand value may not directly increase revenue, and in the short-term there may even be a non-revenue goal behind the branding push. This indirect approach may seem like circuitous path to increased revenue, but the ultimate goal is the same: Making money for the company.

In Coca-Cola's case, this investment has paid off. In fact, Interbrand lists Coca-Cola as one of the most valuable brands in the world. The brand itself has a sense of value, and is easily worth hundreds of billions of dollars. In many ways, the brand identity of Coca-Cola is worth far more than the sum of its products.

Companies are always looking for way to improve the value of their brand. This may take the form of investments in advertising and marketing, or through partnerships that create a better public perception of their brand. Brand value is a form of value unto itself, and it's an important one to consider when it comes to opportunities in business development.

PRODUCT VALUE

Some kinds of value don't create economic value or brand value, but may increase the intrinsic utility of a product or service. Enhancing this value allows you to increase price, attract new customers, and retain a greater share of your existing customers. This type of value is called product value.

There are many kinds of business opportunities where there isn't a direct benefit in terms of revenue or profit, and where there will be little or no impact on the brand. Instead, the opportunity presents a way to improve the product itself. Providing a better product creates a form of value all by itself.

Enhancing product value might enable a company to raise their prices, foster a more loyal relationship with customers, or open the door to a new segment of quality-obsessed customers. Apple's ongoing refinements and new iterations of core products are good examples of this. Product value allows companies to think about value in a new way that is completely separate from economic or brand value.

AUDIENCE VALUE

Does an opportunity help to increase a company's exposure have value? What about a deal that could expand the potential customer base? These might not create immediate economic value, but clearly it creates some form of potential value. This is called audience value, and it plays a key role in many industries.

Most notably, audience value drives the entire publishing industry. Advertisers hope to reach customers through companies with wide audience exposure, such as websites, TV channels, radio, and printed media. By providing access to a large pool of viewers, listeners, and readers, these companies bring audience value to the opportunity, and to create economic value for themselves in the process.

OPTION VALUE

What happens when an opportunity creates a form of value that may not be recognized immediately, but opens the door to something in the future? This is called option value. Opportunities for option value happen all the time, but they can be easy to miss if you don't know what you're looking for.

What does an option value opportunity look like? Let's take a look at an example.

When Apple released the iPhone 4S in 2010, it was exclusively available on two mobile carriers — AT&T and Verizon — cutting smaller providers out of the picture. Sprint soon made a deal with Apple to offer the iPhone 4S to their customers, but it came with a serious condition. To offer the new phone to their customers, Sprint had to guarantee $4 billion in sales to Apple.

Looking at this deal from the context of economic value, it doesn't make much sense. The idea that Sprint would be able to sell $4 billion worth of new iPhones seems insane. Even on paper, the best-case scenario was still a loss for Sprint. This wasn't even a situation where Sprint would be the exclusive provider of the new phone. The deal only allowed them to compete with the other carriers who offered it. At the same time, Sprint was only valued at around $8 billion, meaning that they were risking half of the worth of the entire company just to make the deal happen.

Why would Sprint do something this risky? It turns out that there was a very good reason. At the time, Sprint was struggling for survival, and was likely to be either acquired or put out of business by one of the larger mobile carriers. If they couldn't offer the phones that their customers wanted — like the latest iPhone — they risked losing even more business to the competition. Securing the rights to sell that phone, even if it came at an incredibly high cost, gave them the option value to live another day.

What, Exactly, Is Business Development?

Here's another way of thinking about option value: If you had the opportunity to sell your product or service to Google, but they would only buy it at half the price, would that be worth it? Is it worth slashing the economic value of a product in exchange for the option value of building a relationship with one of the world's most powerful companies?

Maybe that kind of deal would be worth it for you, or maybe not. Business development is all about understanding the different types of value that an opportunity can create, so that you can determine what value you're after, and which opportunities will bring you the value that you need.

Sources Of Value

One final consideration in the definition of business development are the roles that customers, markets, and relationships play in the creation of value. I refer to these as the "sources" of value in a business development opportunity. Let's take a look at each of these in turn.

CUSTOMERS

It's pretty easy to define what a customer is. These are people with whom you have an exchange of value. When you think about economic value, for instance, customers are the people who exchange their money for your products or services. This makes them a source of economic value.

In terms of brand value, on the other hand, customers are the source of the improved perception of your company. Your customers — and sometimes even your potential customers — ultimately determine the value of your brand.

No matter how you define value, customers are a fundamental unit by which value can be measured. An opportunity can be defined by how many customers will be gained, what economic value those customers represent, and what kind of value those customers are looking for.

MARKETS

Markets are where your current and prospective customers live. There are two kinds of markets, and the distinction becomes important when we talk about "entering new markets." These markets may overlap, but it's helpful to look at markets from both angles.

The first definition looks at a market in terms of its geography. For example, a company that serves customers from a brick-and-mortar store in the New York market might realize an opportunity to create long-term value by opening up a store in London. Entering into that market likely means actually going there and setting up shop.

The second way to define a market is by the value mindset of the customers. What types of products, services, and value are customers in that market looking for? By providing those customers with the things they value, you are entering that market.

Consider the pet-owners market. Customers who live in that market are people who own cats, dogs, fish, birds, and other animals. A company like Petco sells to customers who live in the pet-owners market. They sell dog food, cat litter, and all the other products and services that create value for customers who live in that market.

What is an opportunity that a business development person at Petco might face? They might see an opportunity in another market that seems attractive. While doing demographic research, for example, they may have noticed that a large segment of their customers are pale, red-haired guys — just like me. These are guys who need sunscreen and big hats for when they go out to the dog park.

Perhaps this Petco business development person sees an opportunity to move into the lucrative "pale red-haired guy" market. It doesn't matter where those red-haired guys live, it only matters that the products and services on offer match with the needs and values of the red-haired guy mindset. Petco might even decide to put out a line of sunscreens that specifically appeal to customers who live in that pale, red-haired, freckled, burn-up-in-the-sun market — people like me.

The world is filled with opportunities to enter all kinds of markets, but not all of these opportunities are worth taking seriously. A big part of the job of business development is understanding which opportunities to move forward with, and which to ignore. This means vetting these ideas for their long-term value to the company.

RELATIONSHIPS

I like to say that relationships are both the heart and the foundation of long-term value. A company's relationships with its customers, partners, employees, and even the press, are critical to the pursuit of building long-term value. Having a strong respect for these relationships — and understanding how to manage and nurture them — provides a foundation upon which value can flow.

At the same time, it is important to think of these relationships as the heart of long-term value. A relationship isn't a one-time deal, it's an ongoing connection. Maintaining those relationships — keeping that heart beating — is what allows value to continue flowing over that foundation.

Customers, markets, and relationships are the sources of value that drive business development. They also enable the ongoing pursuit of long-term value. But there is another important aspect to business development: People.

The Four Functions Of Business Development

Now that we've defined what business development is, let's take a look at what business development professionals actually do. Who are business development people?

"Business Development" is a job title at many companies, but what it means in practice can vary significantly from one business to another. In one company, it may essentially be a sales job, going out and forging relationships that will lead to more sales and partnerships with other companies. At another company, however, business development might be more of a strategic position, researching which markets are the best to enter, and which customers are the best to attract.

In some companies, business development is the CEO's role. His or her job is deciding on the right direction for the business, creating product and services that will appeal to new customers, and figuring out how to reach customers in new markets. In other companies, the functions and responsibilities of business development are spread out across many different people and positions. There are even companies where an entire team of people have "Business Development" written on their business cards, yet every person on that team has a distinct and unique role.

One might think that it's the sole responsibility of the business development professional to be constantly exploring ways to create value from — and for — customers, markets, and relationships. In reality, business development is a team sport. Perhaps the sales team is out there talking to customers, learning what kinds of value they are looking for and what kinds of markets the company could enter into. A finance team might be tasked with determining if there is enough economic or other value in an opportunity to be worth the time, cost, and risk to pursue. A product-development team might even be called in to figure out how to build a product that will appeal to the customers the company is hoping to attract.

All of these jobs, in their way, play a role in business development.

I have a confession to make: I hate the term "business development." Isn't anyone who works for a business charged — at least in some way — with developing it? No matter what role one plays in a company, there is always an opportunity to create long-term value for that company. Everyone who works at that company, from the janitor to the CEO, should be thinking about how they can create value for the business.

When you look at business development from that perspective, it's easy to see how anyone at the company can play a role in creating long-term value. Business development is something that requires many hands, and many skills. Instead of defining business development by title, it may be helpful to think if it in terms of job function.

Broadly speaking, the job of business development is composed of four essential functions. These are: sales, strategy, partnerships, and relationship management. Let's take a look at these important aspects of the job individually.

Function 1: Sales

Every business development role has some element of sales to it. This isn't necessarily a traditional sales role, however. Business development is unique, because what you're really selling is the idea that this new partnership will bring value to both parties.

In most cases, business development means selling these ideas to another company. Much like traditional sales, this means learning how to navigate that company's organization, and figuring out who at that company is going to be interested in what you have to offer. What you bring to the table might be something tangible, like a product or service, but it can also be something more abstract, like the idea of a partnership.

Selling is an important skill for every business development person to have. At the same time, the style of sales that is needed in business development is a little different from the style needed in most other sales contexts. These differences may seem small, but understanding them is key to the job.

To put this in a sales perspective, business development requires long-cycle sales approach, as opposed to a transactional sales approach. Transactional sales is exactly what it sounds like: the parties involved are making a transaction, like exchanging money for a product. There might not be too much thought or time invested in a transactional purchase, and it usually doesn't need to go through multiple levels of decision-makers and gatekeepers to happen.

Let's say that you wanted to buy a white Calvin Klein t-shirt. You walk into your local clothing store, find the shirt, pay for it, and walk out. This is a purely transactional sale.

Perhaps you decided to go with that particular shirt and brand thanks to an advertisement, but you were going to eventually buy a white t-shirt at some point no matter what. You didn't have to consult with anybody to approve the choice of the t-shirt, the brand, or the clothing store. No one other than you had to approve your purchase. Once the sale was finished, your business with the store was completed.

Selling to an organization is very different, and it calls for a specific approach. Business-to-business sales requires a degree of investigation. For instance, you will often need to track down the decision makers at a given company, working your way through secretaries and other gatekeepers. You may need to learn about that company's "pain points," competitors, and other partnerships. The more information you have, the better, and the only way to get that information is to investigate.

There are many steps in this sales process, and each step takes time. For obvious reasons, we call this process long-cycle sales. Most business development follows the long-cycle sales structure, as it takes an investment of time to identify the right customers and partners, learn about the products they would be interested in buying, and find out if they are interested in what we have to offer.

The challenge for business development is that we aren't selling a commodity. We aren't selling white t-shirts which will be identical at Macy's or at Target. We're selling something bigger. To create opportunities, we need to have consultations with these businesses. Not surprisingly, this kind of sale is called a consultative sale.

Consultative sales generally require many discussions over a period of time. Each discussion involves trying to root out the things that are important to that person or business, looking for reasons that they would be interested in what we have to offer. It also means meeting with gatekeepers — people whose job it is to vet deals and partnerships — as we work our way towards the actual decision makers at the company. Decision makers are the people who have the authority to create agreements, make purchases, and move forward with partnerships, and getting to them always takes time.

This slow-burning, methodical process is a very different approach to that used in many kinds of sales jobs. Understanding how and why long-cycle sales is effective is critical to doing it well.

Function 2: Strategy

Strategy is perhaps one of the most overlooked functions of business development, and yet it is a key aspect of the job. Strategic thinking is essential for figuring out the best paths for reaching new customers, and the best approaches for entering new markets. Other strategic tasks for business developers may involve creating methods for prioritizing growth opportunities, planning the optimal path for pursuing those opportunities, and ensuring that the company is following the right opportunities in the first place.

There is a convenient framework for conveying the strategies of business development: the "Build vs. Buy vs. Partner" model. This means that there are three potential paths every business development opportunity can take

THE BUILD PATH

This means taking an in-house approach, developing everything you need to pursue an opportunity internally. This might mean developing a new product, or it can mean training the staff to go after opportunities on their own. Instead of relying on outside help or purchases, the company builds its own solution to take advantage of the opportunity.

A good example of this would be a startup that builds apps for iPhones. They might look at the idea of building an app for

Android phones as a business development opportunity, increasing their potential customer base to create greater long-term value. The company might already have the engineering talent on staff to develop an Android app, but need additional training and time to learn the intricacies of a new platform. If they decide to invest the time and money needed to create that opportunity, they are taking the build path.

THE BUY PATH

The buy path means purchasing the assets or resources from another company to pursue an opportunity. This could mean buying a product off the shelf or purchasing a license, allowing them to then create a new product or service. It could also mean outsourcing the product to someone else, hiring them to make opportunity a reality. It can even mean buying the outsourcing company itself.

Consider our iPhone app developer example. They recognize the opportunity to build an Android version of one of their most popular apps, but they lack the right people and skills to do it in-house. Rather than invest in the time and training it will take to get their engineers to master building apps for Android, they decide to outsource the work to a firm that already builds Android apps. If they like that company's work and the app finds a market, the iPhone app maker may even decide to purchase them outright, bringing their talent in-house.

THE PARTNER PATH

When you work with another company to mutually benefit from an opportunity together, you're following the partner path. There are tons of examples of partnerships in business development, and I'll be going into these in more detail later. The important thing to keep in mind is that partnership is only one of many options available in business development.

It's not uncommon for people to associate business development with partnerships. This limits the options for pursuing long-term value. In many cases, partnerships aren't the best approach to take. Having said that, partnerships can have some significant advantages for the right business development opportunities, and they deserve a deeper examination.

Function 3: Partnerships

While it is true that partnerships are only one potential path that business opportunities can take — and that's completely true — it's also important to understand that partnerships are also very common paths for business development to take. It's vital for business development people to understand what drives successful partnerships, how to work with other companies, and how to manage those relationships.

Partnerships are often the best available means for creating long-term value. The upside of partnerships is that they are often the fastest, cheapest, and easiest way to reach new customers and markets. In some situations, they may also be the only way to reach certain opportunities.

On the other hand, there are significant downsides to partnerships. For a start, all partnerships require some kind of compromise. Every partnership requires giving up some degree of value or control to the company you are partnering with. There are always trade-offs and negotiations.

When two companies decide to work together towards a common goal, both of them will expect to get something of value out of the deal. While shared economic value is often the focus of these arrangements, that's not always the case. There are plenty of examples of successful partnerships built around other kinds of value.

A good example of this is the 2011 partnership between Foursquare and American Express. As a tiny startup, Foursquare clearly saw economic value in the opportunity to build a relationship with a financial services giant like AmEx for building its reputation. AmEx, on the other hand, had a brand reputation as an old and somewhat stodgy company. By partnering with a sexy, hot startup like Foursquare, AmEx hoped to build brand value.

It worked. AmEx suddenly became associated with a young, interesting, technology company, completely transforming the company's image in the process. The partnership has also helped Foursquare to survive as a mobile brand, something many of their competitors failed to do.

On the other hand, working with a partner also means giving up full control of the opportunity. This may mean taking actions that don't directly benefit your company, or agreeing to ideas or strategies that are less than ideal for the sake of the partnership. Partnerships require compromise, and that can be a problem.

A few years ago, I was at a business event hosted by a Fortune 500 company. The CEO was there, and over lunch someone asked him about managing all the partnerships that his company had internationally. He replied "If I could do it all myself, we wouldn't have partners."

That's an interesting comment from a couple of different angles. On one hand, he's recognizing the inherent compromise of partnerships. If he could do it all himself, why wouldn't he? Why would his company give up all that money and other value? Why would he give up the control of how those opportunities were pursued? Why hand someone else the reins if you don't have to?

On the other hand, he's also recognizing that he and his company can't do it all. Partnerships open doors. They make it eas-

What, Exactly, Is Business Development?

ier to find new opportunities, and to pursue more opportunities together than you could alone. The trade-off is clear.

It's also important to note that there are many different types of partnership, and several different reasons to partner with another company. Let's take a look at a few of these.

DISTRIBUTION PARTNERSHIPS

This is also known as a channel partnership. These arrangements come together when one company has access to a market that another company is looking to connect with. The partnership provides both companies with access to that market, often with both partners splitting the financial and brand benefits.

A great example of this was when high-end fashion designer Isaac Mizrahi partnered with discount retail chain Target, bringing out a new line of clothing specifically for Target shoppers. This is a great example of a distribution partnership. Target has access to a large customer base that normally couldn't afford Mizrahi's products. At the same time, Mizrahi's high-end label gives Target both a boost to their brand and a unique edge over their retail competition.

PRODUCT PARTNERSHIPS

When two companies work together to either create a new product, or enhance an existing product, this is called a product partnership. My favorite examples of product partnerships often come from the food world, where delicious combinations of existing products are combined together to create something brand new.

One recent example of this is the partnership between Doritos and Taco Bell, resulting in the launch of the Doritos Locos Tacos. For the uninitiated, the Doritos Locos Taco is essentially a standard Taco Bell taco, but with a shell formed from

Doritos chips. Depending on how you think about it, this is either a work of genius or absolutely disgusting. As a product partnership, however, the results are hard to ignore. The Doritos Locos Taco has generated record sales for Taco Bell while providing a tremendous amount of brand exposure for Doritos.

BRAND PARTNERSHIP

When two companies work together to jointly promote and cross-promote their products and services, there can be serious benefits for both. This kind of arrangement is called a brand partnership.

A great example of this is the ongoing partnership between McDonald's and Parker Brothers, the makers of the board game Monopoly. McDonald's frequently runs a promotion where Monopoly-branded game pieces are included on packages of French fries and sodas. Those game pieces contain a wide array of prizes, providing McDonald's with a great way to generate excitement and buzz about their products — something that's easier said than done with a brand as established as theirs. Connecting their foods with a beloved, family-oriented game is also very much on brand, reinforcing the idea that McDonald's is a place that families can enjoy together.

What about Parker Brothers? This partnership provides a rare opportunity for a board game dating back to 1903 to become relevant in the minds of a new generation. People who might never think to play Monopoly now have an opportunity to play a version of the game just by going out for a burger and fries. They might even win a prize, creating an even stronger positive association with the game's brand.

When you think about partners, it's important to think about the types of value that you are looking to create. Any given partnership can create many different forms of value. Those partnerships can also combine different kinds of value, allowing both partners to benefit in ways that matter to them.

While it is true that the Isaac Mizrahi partnership with Target is a great example of a channel partnership, it was also a product partnership. That collaboration resulted in the creation of a new line from Mizrahi, and a new kind of product for Target to sell that didn't exist before. Along the same lines, the Doritos and Taco Bell product partnership can also be seen as a brand partnership, with the novelty of the product creating serious pop culture buzz. One can even see the McDonald's and Monopoly brand partnership as a distribution partnership, with McDonald's providing a version of the game across the world.

These complexities make it absolutely essential to be mindful when entering into a partnership with another company. What are the reasons for this partnership to happen? What types of value are you looking to get from it? Are you willing to share that value with your potential partner? Do they have the right customer base, products, or brand to generate the long-term value your company is looking for?

By thinking about these questions, it becomes much easier to identify the right partners for your company.

Function 4: Relationship Management

Business development people must know how to build and manage relationships with customers, partners, employees, and other people who interact with the business. Relationship management is a critical skill, as these relationships are both the foundation and the heart of creating long-term value.

What are some of the skills that help to build strong relationships? All good relationships require two fundamental things. The first is a strong foundation of trust, respect, and integrity.

The second is an exchange of value, where both sides feel like there is a good reason to be in the relationship.

It's important to understand that a business relationship isn't the same thing as a friendship. It's easy to confuse a friendly relationship, or simply being liked by the person we're talking to, with a business relationship. In reality, it is far more important to share a common foundation of mutual trust, respect, and integrity than it is to have a friendly rapport. Strong, mutually beneficial partnerships can happen even if the people at the negotiating table can't stand each other.

Don't get me wrong: Being nice, fun, and friendly is a good place to start when forging relationships. For the business relationship to work — and to create long-term value — getting along on a personal level just isn't enough. Good relationships DO NOT require being friends with the other party.

These relationships also don't require one party to always say "Yes" to a deal, even when it doesn't make sense for them to do so. Relationships in business are often about finding the balance between toeing your own company's line and advocating on behalf of your customer or partner. Being able to do that effectively requires the ability to say "No" when something is not going to create value for your company.

A strong business relationship that is built around trust, respect, and integrity enables both sides to balance their needs with those of their partners. This allows both sides to get the value they need from the relationship.

CHAPTER 3

Business Development Strategies

In this section, we're going to examine the core strategies of business development. We're going to learn new ways of thinking about opportunities, and we're going to take a look at a four-step process for evaluating opportunities and comparing their long-term value. We're also going to discuss the right ways to go after those opportunities once you have decided to move forward.

To start, I want to introduce a company to you called Widget-Co. Maybe you've heard of them? Probably not, because I just made them up.

WidgetCo is a mid-sized manufacturer of widgets, which are a core part of the inner workings of grandfather clocks. At a recent all-hands meeting of the company, an engineer on the product team made an off-hand comment about how she was able to fix her wristwatch using a WidgetCo Model A34 widget. This surprised many people on the staff, because Widget-Co widgets have never been used in the wristwatch industry. In fact, their widgets had never been used for anything other than grandfather clocks.

Having heard this, the company's CEO now suspects that there is an opportunity for WidgetCo to sell their widgets into the wristwatch industry. The CEO then turns to you, as the newly hired head of business development, to investigate the potential of this opportunity.

This is what business development is all about. An idea for an opportunity has been proposed, and the thought is that it could create long-term value for the company. Now, it's the business development team's job to figure out if this is a viable opportunity to pursue, who the potential partners are, what the long-term value might be, and — if everything in the opportunity lines up — how to go after it.

How does a business development person actually determine if the opportunity is viable? Let's take a look at how this process works. It just takes four easy steps.

Step 1: Identify The Opportunity

Usually, this means thinking about your business and identifying ways to create more value from customers, markets, and relationships. It also means asking questions of your business. Here are a few examples:

- Are there any places where your products and services have a gap relative to your competitors?

- Are there products, features, or services that your customers have been asking for, and which you can now offer to them?

- Are there areas where your competitors are stronger than you? How could you fill the gap?

- Is there something your company could be doing to better support existing customers?

- How can your company enter into a new market to reach new customers?

What, Exactly, Is Business Development?

Identifying opportunities is the easy part. If anything, business development teams are overwhelmed with ideas for opportunities. There are millions of ideas floating around in the ether, creating countless possibilities for even the smallest company.

Business development ideas can come from anywhere. They can come from the business development team, the sales force, the CEO, the janitor, or even the janitor's mother. Anyone can have a good idea for an opportunity. In many companies, it's also relatively easy to get those ideas heard. The real challenge is understanding how to weed out the good ideas from the bad ones.

Frankly, business development ideas are a dime a dozen. Most business development people, CEOs, and entrepreneurs have more ideas for opportunities than they could ever use. These ideas might be interesting, or even uniquely compelling, but that doesn't mean that they will ultimately result in the creation of long-term value for the company. Making this kind of determination is a core part of the business development professional's job description.

How does a business development team determine which opportunities are the right ones to pursue, and which ones should be completely avoided? Let's return to our friends at WidgetCo for a moment.

An engineer discovered that a product designed for grandfather clocks may have some utility and appeal in the wristwatch market. This presents an opportunity to sell an existing product to a new type of customer. Since WidgetCo has only ever sold to the grandfather clock industry, and has never sold to the wristwatch industry, this creates the potential to sell to an entirely new market.

It certainly sounds like it might be worthwhile opportunity. But how can WidgetCo's business development team prove that this is an idea worth pursuing? To move the idea forward, they need to assess the opportunity.

Step 2: Assessing The Opportunity

Now that we've learned how to identify an opportunity, it's time to learn how to assess an opportunity. This means understanding the pros and cons of the opportunity, and it often means assigning a numerical or financial value to some aspects of it.

No matter what kind of value we're looking to create from an opportunity — economic value, brand value, product value — there is always a way to quantify it. Being able to assign a number to those values is extremely important, as it allows you to fairly compare opportunities against each other. Every schoolkid knows this idea: It's comparing apples to apples, not apples to oranges.

One of the most useful ways to start the process of sizing up an opportunity is creating a back-of-the-envelope calculation. This is just a sketch of the idea, something that can be scribbled out on a napkin or on the margins of meeting handout. It's a simple, quick calculation that only serves to give us a rough sense of how big an opportunity could be.

Back-of-the-envelope calculations aren't meant to be definitive assessments. They are just quick-and-dirty ballpark estimates that serve as the first test of an opportunity's viability. If an opportunity doesn't seem viable in a back-of-the-envelope calculation, it probably isn't worth pursuing. At the same time, just because an opportunity looks promising after this calculation doesn't mean it's a guaranteed winner, either.

Let's take a look at how a back-of-the-envelope assessment might work for our friends at WidgetCo.

As we know, WidgetCo is looking at the idea of selling their widgets to the wristwatch industry. They only have experience selling to the grandfather clock industry, and don't have any first-hand experience with the wristwatch market. So, how can

WidgetCo get a rough idea for how big this opportunity is? That's right! It's time for a back-of-the-envelope calculation.

As the head of the business development team, the calculation itself falls to you. You decide that a good way to start is by thinking about the overall size of the wristwatch industry, and then narrow down the possibilities to create an estimate of how many widgets your company could sell to wristwatch makers. To do this, you will need to as close as you can using a mix of real numbers, estimates, and assumptions.

After some research, you learn that there are 150 million watches sold in the United States each year. How many widgets does that equal? According to your engineers, four standard watch gears can be replaced by just two WidgetCo widgets. These widgets are also less expensive and more efficient than standard wristwatch gears, creating a significant selling point. After further investigation, it seems like a reasonable assumption that most watches on the market could benefit from this two-widget solution.

You now have two key pieces of data to work with: 150 million watches; and two widgets per watch. This means that there is a potential for 300 million widgets to be sold into the wristwatch market per year. If each widget wholesales for $0.43 each, this means that the total addressable market for the opportunity is roughly $129 million.

The total addressable market is a term that describes the complete potential opportunity. It assumed that you are able to sell your widgets to 100% of all wristwatch makers, and that every watch they sell has two WidgetCo widgets inside. In reality, this kind of result never happens, but it does help to establish a hypothetical upper boundary for the opportunity.

There's even a name for this kind of thinking: The 1% of China Problem. When people talk about addressable markets, they often enter into their calculations with somewhat unrealistic expectations. "If we could only sell our products to 1% of China, we would have 13 million customers!" Or course, actually reaching 1% of the total addressable Chinese market is still an incredibly tricky thing to do.

For WidgetCo, a more realistic assumption might be reaching 7% of the total addressable wristwatch market. This could be achieved by creating relationships with a handful of major players in the wristwatch game, and is completely accomplishable for a company with a small business development team the size of WidgetCo's. It's still an assumption, but one that is far more plausible than aiming for 100% of the market.

Let's take a look at this calculation:

- 150 million watches sold
- 2 widgets per watch
- $0.43 per widget
- 7% of the total market
- Total opportunity = $9 million per year

This is a true back-of-the-envelope calculation. You did some quick research, made a few basic assumptions, and did a little simple math to figure out the ballpark value of the opportunity. It doesn't need to be perfect — and the results shouldn't be taken too seriously — but it did give you something to start with.

With this calculation in hand, you can now determine whether or not you want to explore this opportunity any further. Perhaps a $9 million opportunity presents an enormous potential for WidgetCo, doubling the average annual sales they make from the slow-growing grandfather clock industry. On the other hand, maybe WidgetCo's dominance on the global widget market means that they don't even get out of bed for less than $50 million. In that case, an opportunity worth a mere $9 million gets thrown out of the window, and the company moves on to something else.

A back-of-the-envelope calculation allows the business development team to take a step back, consider the size of the opportunity, and think about the overall value of the opportunity for the company. By going through this process with every opportunity, it becomes much easier to give priority to the best opportunities.

ASSESSING THE RESOURCE COST

The size of the opportunity is only one part of the assessment, however. Once we know how big the opportunity is, the next step is to determine what it would realistically cost to pursue that opportunity. This is called "assessing resources," and there are many different angles that need to be considered.

- **Product:** Does the company have the assets and expertise to create the product? Are they lacking something critical, such as engineering talent or manufacturing resources?

- **Distribution:** Does the company have a way to sell the product? Does it lack the means to reach those potential customers?

- **Brand:** Does it make sense for the company to enter into this particular industry? Will moving into this market change or hurt the brand in the eyes of its customers?

The first two angle are fairly intuitive, but the third might require an explanation. Does it really matter all that much for a brand to enter into a new market?

Think about Godiva chocolate. If you're like me, the name summons up concepts like luscious chocolate treats, premium quality, and rich flavor. That's not an accident. Godiva's whole brand is built around communicating those ideas to their customers.

What you probably didn't think of was "Cream of Split Pea soup." But perhaps you should have. In 1967, Campbell's — yes, the soup maker — acquired Godiva, launching the brand's rapid growth in the U.S. market. Does that affect your impression of Godiva — or dare I say, put a bit of a bad taste in your mouth?

Growing up, I always thought that Godiva was a premium chocolatier, an idea reinforced by their European-style, luxury-focused marketing. So, when I learned that they were owned by the same company that made plain old canned soups, it completely changed my perception of Godiva chocolates. It took away brand value from Godiva, at least for me.

You can think about a lot of different kinds of resources this way. There are countless examples of the resources and trade-offs that can come into play when considering an opportunity. Another prime example is opportunity cost.

In most business development situations, you will have many more ideas for opportunities than you have resources to pursue. Any time you decide to pursue one opportunity over another, it also means that you are giving up the opportunity to develop the idea that you didn't go with. The more limited your resources are, the higher those opportunity costs become. Investing into Opportunity A often means giving up on Opportunity B, at least for the moment.

Another factor in making this kind of decision is competition. Is the market you are looking into filled with a ton of deeply entrenched competitors? Are you going to be fighting for customers against other companies? What advantages do those companies have over yours? On the other hand, you might be looking at a largely untapped market, with no real competition to worry about.

There is a huge difference between entering into a crowded market and discovering a "white space" opportunity. Depending on the situation, the level of competition can either erode or increase your projections for the cost of entering into the market, as well as the potential for generating long-term value.

Every business is different, and every opportunity presents a unique set of pros and cons for that business. These factors need to be weighed as the opportunity is developed, and balanced against the costs, resources required, and risks. There are no one-size-fits-all answers to these questions, and it's the job of the business development team to consider all of these factors as they create an assessment of an opportunity.

Let's take another look at our WidgetCo example. As the leader of the business development team, you've estimated the idea of moving into the wristwatch market to be a $9 million opportunity. But from a resource standpoint, what would it take to turn this idea into a value-generating reality?

Consider what we know:

- According to WidgetCo's engineers, there is no need to change the product. Existing A34 widgets — already being sold to makers of grandfather clocks — were able to replace wristwatch gears without modification.

- According to the product team, there is excess capacity on the manufacturing line, so there should be no opportunity cost in terms of being able to meet demand.

- At present, however, there is no means for distributing widgets to wristwatch makers.

That last point could be a problem. The WidgetCo sales team has only ever sold to manufacturers in the grandfather clock industry. In order to sell to wristwatch makers, WidgetCo's sales team needs to identify the wristwatch companies who might be most receptive to adopting widgets. They then need to penetrate those organizations to find key gatekeepers and decision makers. Finally, they need to build relationships at those companies, making the case for WidgetCo's product.

In other words, WidgetCo needs to launch a long-cycle sales process. That takes time. For that $9 million opportunity to make sense for WidgetCo, the costs of starting up a new sales cycle need to be weighed against the long-term value it would generate. To get a meaningful answer, we need to consider other ways that the distribution issue could be resolved.

Step 3: Evaluate The Paths

Now that we've drawn some lines around the benefits and limitations associated with an opportunity, it's time to start thinking about the many ways that opportunity could become a reality. In most cases, a company will need to take some kind of action in order to bring an opportunity to fruition.

This brings us back to the Build vs. Buy vs. Partner framework we discussed in Chapter 2. This structure allows us to create multiple potential resolutions for the various roadblocks and problems an opportunity presents. Let's take a look at each of these in turn.

OPTION 1 — THE BUILD PATH

What will it take to pursue the opportunity entirely in-house? If our company lacks the resources we need, what would it take to fill in those gaps?

OPTION 2 — THE BUY PATH

Can we outsource the things we need to enable us to pursue the opportunity? Is there something we can purchase off the shelf that we can plug into our solution, allowing us to move forward with the opportunity more quickly or easily?

OPTION 3 — THE PARTNER PATH

Are there any other companies that we could work with to jointly pursue this opportunity? What are the pros and cons of working with each potential partner?

There's also a hidden, fourth option that we haven't talked about: Doing nothing.

Sometimes, an opportunity just isn't worth it. Maybe it looks promising in the beginning, but as you learn more about the market or uncover hidden costs, it becomes clear that the potential long-term value is much less than you initially thought. Doing nothing in that situation might be the smartest move.

An opportunity that is worth $9 million per year, like our WidgetCo example, might be a game changer for the company, or it could be a drop in the bucket. If WidgetCo is a $50 billion company, is an additional $9 million a year really worth thinking about? In business development, it's important to remember that not every opportunity is a good one. If an opportunity doesn't make sense to pursue, you can always decide to do nothing.

Once you have found an opportunity that you are confident is worth pursuing, and you have backed this assessment up with the best data you can find, it's time to start moving forward. What paths can a business development team take to develop this opportunity?

Let's consider the options available for WidgetCo.

If WidgetCo decides to move forward with the Build Path, they might decide to train their existing sales team to sell to watchmakers. Having only ever sold to grandfather clock makers, they will need to build relationships in that new market from scratch. The sales team will need to go out and start meeting with these potential customers, working their way through each organization, learning what people in those companies are looking for, and identifying the people who are ready to buy WidgetCo's products.

Creating this kind of long-cycle sales structure could take a long time to set up, but it is also a relatively inexpensive approach. In WidgetCo's case, the Build Path would take about 18 months and around $1 million to get going. The sales staff will need to travel to trade shows, meet customers across the country, and spend time getting to know the people in the wristwatch industry to establish relationships. Only after all of these things have been done — building a foundation of trust, respect, and integrity along the way — can WidgetCo's sales team bring these potential customers to the bargaining table to talk about multimillion dollar deals.

The second option for WidgetCo is the Buy Path. This would likely mean hiring a new sales team made up of veterans of the wristwatch sales industry. The people on this new sales team would already have existing relationships with wristwatch makers, dramatically reducing training costs and the time needed to get up to speed. WidgetCo would, however, need to take on some additional expenses in the form of salaries, benefits, bonuses, and recruiting fees.

For this option, WidgetCo believes that it could have the sales team ready to go within three months. The company would start seeing a return on their investment in a quarter of the time as the Build Path. At the same time, the costs associated with launching this new sales team will be much higher. WidgetCo predicts this will take around $5 million.

The third option is the Partner Path. In this scenario, Widget-Co would work with another company to cross-sell widgets along with their existing product line. This allows WidgetCo to take advantage of their partner company's expertise in the wristwatch market, but it comes at the cost of splitting the revenue from those sales.

What, Exactly, Is Business Development?

As it turns out, WidgetCo does have one promising potential partner. StrapCo is the leading maker of high-quality leather wristwatch straps. As a result, they already have relationships with all the big names in the wristwatch industry. If StrapCo's sales team also sold WidgetCo's widgets, mentioning the benefits every time they spoke to a new or existing customer in the wristwatch industry, both companies could benefit from the increased sales.

How does a partnership like this take shape? WidgetCo's business development team needs to get a foot in the door at StrapCo, then find the right people to engage in a partnership discussion. It will take some time for the details of the agreement to be hammered out, but the entire process should be quite inexpensive. WidgetCo believes the partnership could be ready to go within six months.

Of course, partnerships come at a cost. For every widget StrapCo sells on WidgetCo's behalf, they will take a piece of that value. WidgetCo is willing to give their partner a 30% share of the revenue for every widget they sell. In this $9 million per year opportunity, WidgetCo would be giving up $2.7 million every year to StrapCo.

Build, Buy and Partner are three viable paths for pursuing an opportunity. The next step is actually deciding on which path is the best for your company.

Step 4: Make A Decision

Making a decision might seem like a relatively straightforward thing to do, particularly when compared to the other steps. But it isn't always so simple. Every company, and every individual decision maker — from the front-line business development person to the CEO — has a different way of thinking about and deciding on the right action to take.

One person might make this decision from a purely financial perspective, weighing expenses and risks against the options that present the most potential value or require the least upfront costs. Another person might make their decision based on a gut feeling, their business intuition, and their own risk tolerance. How these decisions play out, and what shape an opportunity ultimately takes, depends on the personalities of the people tasked with making the final call.

That said, each of these options do follow a predictable pattern. Knowing how these paths tend to work can help in coming to the right decision. Let's take a look at how these play out:

BUILD PATH

This is usually the slowest way to enter a market, but it does provide you with the most control over the outcome. Building your own solution enables you to control own destiny, and to retain full control over your costs, products, and revenues. Any value created by this opportunity belongs to you, and you won't have to split it with anyone else.

Pros: Most Control. **Cons:** Slowest path.

BUY PATH

This can be the riskiest and most expensive option to pursue, but it can also be the fastest. It requires that you take someone else's solution — their skills, their product, their services, or even their entire company — and plug it into your opportunity. (A quick side note: Business development can often become a gateway drug for "corporate development," which can often mean mergers and acquisitions. Buying another company is one of the more extreme examples of the Buy Path.)

Pros: Fastest path. **Cons:** Risky and expensive.

PARTNER PATH

Compromise is the defining trait of partnership. The Partner Path is often a mix of pros and cons, with every partnership being unique. Partnerships also involve the idea of "shared risk, shared reward," allowing both parties to hedge the upside and downside of the opportunity. Mitigating the risk of pursuing an opportunity can be a strong incentive, but it also means giving up some of the value the opportunity generates. The success of a partnership also depends on the nature of the agreement, which party has the most leverage in negotiating the deal, and how well the partnership itself works over time.

Pros: Reduced risk. **Cons:** Reduced value.

Now that we've outlined these options, let's take a look at what these could mean for WidgetCo.

WidgetCo's first option is the Build Path. Training their existing sales team to sell into the wristwatch industry would take 18 months and cost around $1 million before seeing a return on that investment. While this means a slow entry into the wristwatch market, WidgetCo would retain the most money from the opportunity when compared to the other options. At the end of the first full sales cycle, WidgetCo would bring in $8 million, and then $9 million every year after.

The second option for WidgetCo is the Buy Path. Hiring another sales team that is already familiar with the wristwatch industry would allow WidgetCo to enter into the market within 3 months. This is also the most expensive option, however, costing $5 million. This only leaves $4 million in profit after the first sales cycle for WidgetCo, but returns the full $9 million every year after.

Finally, WidgetCo has the Partner Path to consider. This means partnering with a company like StrapCo, which already has the relationships needed to sell into the wristwatch industry.

It also means that WidgetCo would give up a piece of the action, with 30% of the revenue going to their partner. StrapCo could start selling widgets within six months, but at the cost of $2.7 million per year. This leaves $6.3 million per year for WidgetCo.

What needs to be considered when weighing these options? The Build and Buy Paths both require an upfront investment of several million dollars, but after that initial cost is paid, WidgetCo gains $9 million every year. As long as the costs are stable and the size of the opportunity remains the same, those early expenses are simply sunk costs.

With a partnership, however, WidgetCo would have to keep paying $2.7 million every year to StrapCo. That cost recurs every year that the partnership is in place. While there was no substantial upfront investment, WidgetCo stands to lose out on tens of millions in revenue over the long term. If WidgetCo believes the opportunity to be too financially risky, however, partnering with StrapCo might make the most sense. After all, WidgetCo has no relationships in the wristwatch industry, and no expertise in selling into it.

There are also variations and hybrid versions of these options. Perhaps it makes more sense to work with a partner at the start, gauging market demand in a low-risk way. If it goes well, it will always be possible to build an in-house sales team later. It's even possible that a partnership with StrapCo ultimately results in WidgetCo buying the company, with the strength of the sales team being one of the core assets.

It's even possible that none of these options seem like a good fit, and that the best course of action is to go back to the start of the process. Maybe the indecision is a sign that Widget-Co needs to do more due diligence. Is the wristwatch market really worth moving into at all? Is the market growing? Is trying to move into that market a better use of resources than some other opportunity, such as expanding into other kinds of wall-mounted clocks?

There are any number of ways to pursue an opportunity. It's the job of the business development person to look at opportunities from all angles, gathering the best information so that these decisions are as well-informed as possible.

CHAPTER 4

Tactical Business Development In Action

Now that we've talked about the general strategies of business development, it's time to talk about pursuing opportunities on a tactical level. Specifically, we're going to explore how partnership opportunities work.

This may surprise you, but the tactics for creating a partnership are actually pretty similar to those used in making a new sale. On a tactical level, selling the idea of a partnership is fundamentally no different than selling any product or service. Many of the principles we're about to cover for partnerships could just as easily apply to any kind of sales.

Creating a partnership requires an understanding of how to navigate your way through the organization of another company. This allows you to figure out who at that company will care about what you have to offer. It also requires the ability to talk to those gatekeepers and decision makers in a way that allows them to see the value that your idea could bring to them. In sales, that value comes in the form of a product or service, and in business development it comes in the form a partnership.

As with any process, forging a partnership isn't something you can rush though. These relationships are formed over several stages, with each stage requiring its own specific tactics. Let's take a look at this process.

Step 1: Find A Contact

Before you can create a partnership, you need to think about which companies would make good partners. Not all companies will be a good match for your needs, and each one will bring a unique set of characteristics to the table. One company might bring a great brand value to a partnership, for instance, but have limited financial resources or distribution channels.

Thinking about the kind of value that you are after, and the resources that you lack, will help you determine the best companies to approach about a partnership. For a partnership to work, your resources and needs should be complementary, allowing both companies to benefit from the opportunity.

In many situations, there will be multiple companies that could be good partners. It's important to narrow this list down to only those businesses that truly make sense for the partnership you have in mind.

- If you are looking for a distribution partnership, which companies have the best access to the customers and market that your company wants to enter into?

- If you are looking to gain brand value by associating your company with a larger organization, which companies have a reputation that would help to boost your brand?

- If you're looking for a product partnership, which companies have products and services that would best complement those offered by your company?

As you create a list of potential partners, it's a good idea to start thinking about those companies' organizational structures. At each of those businesses, who is most likely to be receptive to the idea you have for a partnership?

Figuring out the right person to talk to is partially a logistical and research exercise — who is in charge of what, and how do you contact them — but it is also a matter of understanding what motivates people. This means tapping into two key types of motivation a person can have.

The first is their role within the context of the organization. Are there people within the company whose job it is to evaluate partnerships? In a distribution-type partnership, you might need to talk to someone in that company's business development team.

In other cases, it might be a better strategy to talk to someone in sales, product development, engineering, or manufacturing. It's important that the person you talk to has a vested interest in what you have to offer, because their job duties are strongly tied to the type of partnership you are proposing.

The other type of motivation is individual. Is there someone in the organization that has a personal reason to respond to your inquiries, discuss your ideas, and promote a partnership? Even if their personal motivation is only indirectly related to their job function, it can still be a valuable tool for generating a response and getting you in the door.

Getting in the door with a company can be more challenging that you might expect. Let's take a look at the different kinds of contact. If you have spent any time working in sales, these concepts should be familiar to you.

COLD CALLS

Going in "cold" means that you have no prior exposure to the person that you are trying to reach. You're reaching out to them blindly. Maybe you found them through an internet search, or saw them on LinkedIn.

While cold emails and cold calls are viable options, they are also the most challenging way to get someone to respond. Unless the value that you have to offer is obvious to them, they may simply ignore your messages. It is possible to "warm up" these cold contacts, but it takes time and persistence.

WARM CALLS

A "warm" contact means that you have some kind of connection with this person already. Perhaps there is a mutual acquaintance who can introduce you to the right person at the company. Is there a trade show, conference, or networking event where you can introduce yourself to someone at that company? Reliably finding warm leads requires building a network, socializing with people from other companies and industries, and getting to know people at all levels of an organization. This takes time and effort, but it's an investment that usually pays off.

People are far more willing to respond if they have some degree of connection to you already. This isn't limited to real-world contact, either. Simply commenting on someone's blog or replying to something they posted to Twitter can help to warm them to later contact. This is often the first step to getting your foot in the door with them.

Let's apply this idea to WidgetCo's situation.

WidgetCo needs to start a conversation with the people at StrapCo, but none of the people on the sales or business development teams knows anyone who works at StrapCo. After putting out a call to the rest of the staff, however, it turns out that there is a promising lead.

One of WidgetCo's accountants, Sally James, met a StrapCo sales rep at a conference a few months ago. His name is John Samuels, and Sally says that she'll be happy to make an introduction. John may not be the best possible lead, but he is warmest lead WidgetCo has at the moment.

How does WidgetCo start the process of working its way through the StrapCo organization? That's in step two.

Step 2: Get A Meeting

A warm introduction is not a silver bullet. We need to have a good reason for them to want to meet with us in the first place. One of the best ways to generate a compelling reason is to create a "value hypothesis." A value hypothesis is a guess that the value of your partnership idea will be interesting enough for someone at another company to open the door and listen to what you have to say.

Once you have identified a potential contact, it's important to spend some time thinking about what they might find valuable. What you could offer to them that might catch their attention? It doesn't have to be something of mind-blowing value, it just needs to be compelling enough to get them to agree to that first meeting.

This means that it is imperative for you to concisely and clearly communicate that value hypothesis to your contact. No matter how you communicate that message — from making a phone call to sending a tweet — you need to keep it brief and impactful. Think of this as a variation on the "elevator pitch," presenting the strongest possible value hypothesis in four or five sentences.

Why will meeting with you be a valuable use of their time? Is what you have to say all that relevant to them? What do they gain by hearing you out?

People are busy, and just getting someone to open an email from someone they don't know can be a challenge. A strong value hypothesis allows you to quickly demonstrate why meeting with you will be a good use of their time. This means having a clear understanding of why they should meet with you, both personally and organizationally.

Let's look at how WidgetCo can use this approach to get in the door with StrapCo.

WidgetCo has one potential contact on StrapCo's sales team, but we don't yet have strong value hypothesis for starting a conversation about a partnership between the two companies. After workshopping some ideas with other people on the business development team, however, you've crafted an email that might do the trick.

> *Hi John,*
>
> *Thanks for the introduction, Sally. John, it's great to be introduced. I was hoping you could help me connect with someone on the StrapCo team responsible for sales and strategic partnerships.*
>
> *WidgetCo is exploring opportunities to offer our widgets into the watch industry, and we believe there may be opportunities for collaboration. We believe that a partnership between StrapCo and WidgetCo may provide a significant revenue opportunity to both companies.*
>
> *Would you be free to meet next Tues. or Weds. to talk further?*
>
> *— Scott*

Note that the message is short. Within just a few sentences, we have explained why we want to meet, and why our idea is relevant to both John and StrapCo. Let's take a look at the individual elements of the email.

- **Get an introduction:** Because we already have an introduction to John, we're going into this warm. While he may not be the perfect person to talk to at the company, we're at least getting the ball rolling.

- **Know your audience:** Right at the start, we acknowledge that we're not sure who the right contact is. We then ask for his help in getting referred to the right person to talk

What, Exactly, Is Business Development?

to for strategic partnerships. We know that he is in Strap-Co's sales organization, and it's possible that he has some responsibility for driving new sales.

- **Consider their motivations:** As a sales person, John might be interested in bringing new opportunities to the company, and in selling new products to his existing customers. A good partnership with WidgetCo could potentially increase his commissions, boost his bonus, and raise his profile within StrapCo. These all play to John's individual motivations, increasing the chances that he'll want to hear more.

- **Have a value hypothesis:** We introduce the idea of our partnership. We explain the potential for collaboration between WidgetCo and StrapCo, and introduce the notion of significant revenue growth opportunities for both companies. This is also a brand new idea, and a first in the industry. These factors should at least be interesting and novel enough to catch John's interest in hearing more.

- **Keep it concise:** This whole email is only six sentences long. It says everything it needs to, and no more. We're not trying to close the deal here, we're just trying to pique the interest of the one contact we have at StrapCo. All it has to do is get us in the door.

With a message like this, we think we can actually get a meeting with John on the calendar. From there, we need to start building interest at StrapCo in the idea of a partnership.

Step 3: Interest-Building Meetings

Meetings are where the real discussions about partnerships can take place. The more interest and enthusiasm you can generate at these meetings, the more likely a partnership becomes. These early meetings are called, not surprisingly, interest-building meetings.

It's important to remember that the purpose of these meetings isn't to try to close the deal right away. We aren't there yet. All we've managed to do is convince a contact to open a window in their schedule to hear what we have to say. This is the first conversation out of many to come.

Our only goal with these early meetings is to raise their level of interest in our partnership idea. Each time we talk, we want to raise their interest level a little more. A good partnership requires that both sides are excited about the prospect of working together.

This also means that both potential partners need to be able to weigh in with their own ideas. Discussions about what both sides need from the partnership need to be taken seriously. Both sides need to support the idea, and support each other as the partnership takes shape. The more collaborative the process, the more both sides will be able to see the overall value of the partnership.

In these meetings, don't focus exclusively on what's in it for you. Don't focus exclusively on what's in it for them, either. Recognize that these conversations will evolve, and allow ideas from both sides to filter in. To generate long-term value, a sustainable partnership has to make sense for both companies.

Another important aspect of these early meetings is to keep it simple. Coming in with a 50-slide PowerPoint deck or a two-hour product demo isn't a good idea. It's always tempting to try to win someone over with a huge presentation of why your product or service is going to make for a great partnership, but in reality this approach rarely works in your favor.

Instead, spend a little time looking at this opportunity from their point of view. What parts of the collaboration would generate the most interest for them? What ideas might make them want to keep the conversation going? What would a successful partnership look like to them?

Collaborations like this take time. You can't come into a partnership discussion expecting to close the deal after the first discussion. It's likely that the people at that first meeting won't even have the ability to move forward with a deal, even if they wanted to. To establish a partnership, you will need to slowly work your way up through the organization, building both their level of interest and their trust along the way.

Let's look at how this first partnership meeting might play out for WidgetCo.

By reaching out to John at StrapCo's sales team, you've been able to set up a meeting. At the very least, John was interested in hearing more. At the initial meeting, you explained that WidgetCo is looking for a partner in a distribution deal. You think there's a significant market for WidgetCo's widgets as a replacement for those old-fashioned wristwatch gears, bringing down costs for watchmakers. Unfortunately, WidgetCo only knows the grandfather clock market, and needs a distribution partner to start moving into the wristwatch market.

With all this in mind, StrapCo seems like a natural fit. Widget-Co believes that this is a $9 million opportunity, and it represents a substantial new revenue stream for both companies. StrapCo not only gets a slice of the revenue, but they also get a new product to sell to their existing customers. A partnership could offer real product value for StrapCo's customers, creating more loyalty among their existing customers and an interesting selling point when talking to new ones.

By combining WidgetCo's unique product with StrapCo's great access to customers in the wristwatch industry, there is obvious potential for a distribution partnership. There is a clear and compelling partnership opportunity here, with serious product, revenue, and brand value gains for both sides.

John likes what he hears, and says he'll talk to the higher ups at StrapCo about the idea. Case closed? Hardly. John seems to be on board, but he's just one person out of many that you will need to meet, talk to, and negotiate with as the deal moves forward. John's real role here is to help you set up the next meeting with StrapCo's leadership.

These meetings can take time, and you generally shouldn't rush them. Throughout the course of these discussions, the meetings should steadily become more focused on what a partnership between the two companies would actually look like. Ultimately, these conversations will result in the final step: Closing the deal.

Step 4: Closing The Deal

I hate the term "closing the deal." In my experience, there is no such thing as "closing." It's a term that gets thrown around a lot, but what does it really mean in the context of business development? Plenty of people may claim that there's some secret technique or mind game you can use to get the other person to sign on the dotted line, but in reality it doesn't really work that way.

The truth is that "closing tactics" are more hype than reality. The idea that you can adopt a certain posture, use specific kinds of language, or play mind games with people on the other side of the table to force them to agree to a partnership is ludicrous in the real world. It's not real.

Closing is not an event. It's one step out of many in the evolution of a relationship between two companies. As the idea of what a partnership might be slowly takes shape, both sides are steadily working their way towards the end goal of bringing that partnership to market.

If both sides are truly motivated to move forward, the final "closing" stage is really just a matter of getting the details on paper, signing the contracts, and moving the partnership into the market. Closing is a formality.

That's not to say that closing a deal is should be boring. Those final stages of putting a partnership together can feel like running the last few hundred yards of a marathon. But there's nothing magical about those last few steps, because it took 26.2 miles of running to get you there. Closing feels good because it means you made it past the finish line.

As you progress towards closing, it's important to keep a few things in mind.

TIMELINES CAN VARY

Every company has a different process for evaluating partnerships. Legal teams may need to look over every iteration of an agreement, financial people might try to play hardball about revenue shares, and marketing teams could quibble over who has final say in any advertising designs. This is normal, and to be expected.

Coming to an agreement on these details can take weeks or months. Depending on the complexity of the deal and the size of the organizations involved, it can even take years. By factoring this into your expectations, you can avoid a lot of frustration.

KNOW YOUR PRIORITIES, AND STICK TO THEM

As your discussions continue, and you get more specific in your discussions about what a partnership might look like, it's important to have a firm position on the key terms of the deal.

The partnership must provide real value to both sides. If the terms shift to the point where your company isn't getting the level of value that you need, it's essential that you point this out.

When the initial idea for the opportunity first presented itself, that back-of-the-envelope calculation was built on a series of assumptions. In the course of these discussions, those assumptions have probably been challenged. This can fundamentally change the value of the opportunity.

WidgetCo assumed that a 30% revenue share was reasonable, for example, but a partnership for StrapCo might only make sense if that revenue share is 50%. What does this mean for WidgetCo? Does a partnership still make as much sense if it costs $4.5 million per year? That's almost the same amount as it would cost to simply hire a new, wristwatch-industry savvy sales team. Is this partnership with StrapCo still worthwhile?

BE COMFORTABLE WITH COMPROMISE

It's vital to know your own priorities, but it's just as important to anticipate and adjust to the needs and priorities of your potential partner. A willingness to compromise is important in any negotiation, but that doesn't mean there isn't a strategic element to it. Expect to compromise, and have a plan in place before you need to.

Conceding according to a plan requires that you know what your bottom line is. Letting your partner "win" certain parts of the agreement isn't a bad thing in negotiations, as long as you are still getting enough out of the deal to make it worth the effort. Conceding on points that have less value to you, and give more value to your partner, allows you to compromise comfortably. This can help keep negotiations friendly, and helps both sides to feel like they are getting the best possible deal.

What, Exactly, Is Business Development?

YOU CAN ALWAYS WALK AWAY

It's important to know when to hold 'em, but it's even more important to know when to fold 'em. The more alternatives you have in any negotiation, the stronger you will be. It's easy to get stuck in the mindset that everything depends on making the current partnership happen. Remember to keep things in perspective.

In business development, there is always another potential partnership around the corner. Each new opportunity might will have plenty of paths for pursuing it. Prioritizing your opportunities allows you to go into a negotiation with the confidence to know that if you are no longer getting the value that you need from the partnership, you can always walk away from it. No partnership is always better than a bad partnership.

Now that we're talking about the closing stages of a deal, let's take a look at what happened with WidgetCo.

After several meetings, StrapCo was interested in exploring a partnership. They liked the idea of offering a more varied product line to their customers. Unfortunately, they also felt that deal didn't make sense on their side unless they could get a 50% revenue share from selling WidgetCo's widgets. After some internal discussion, WidgetCo decided that giving up that extra 20% could work, but only if StrapCo agreed to an exclusivity deal preventing any other widget makers from selling their products through StrapCo.

It took weeks of complex negotiations, with compromises on both sides, but at the end WidgetCo and StrapCo were able to hammer out a deal that they both felt comfortable with. WidgetCo is finally poised to enter into a new market, and both companies are excited about the new source of long-term value the deal represents.

Congratulations WidgetCo business development team!

You've successfully closed your first deal. Now it's time to get back to work, and to start looking for the next big opportunity in the wild world of widgets.

Conclusion

Hopefully, this book has helped you demystify what business development is really all about. It's a method for pursuing growth in companies, and for creating long-term value for an organization. Business development professionals need to always be thinking about ways to create value and generate growth for their companies. It's a game that you play over and over again, constantly improving, but never completely mastering.

Playing the business development game means having a clear vision for how opportunities and partnerships work. Knowing how this process works allows you pursue any deal you want. It also allows you to strengthen your bottom line, and build exceptional growth for your company.

If you like what you've read here, check out my website at StartOfTheDeal.com. Happy business developing!

About The Author

 **Scott Pollack** is weirdly obsessed with business development. He's spent his career leading BD efforts at companies of all shapes and sizes — from fast-paced startups like WeWork to global behemoths like American Express. Today, Scott is the Founder and CEO of Firneo.

Made in the USA
Coppell, TX
22 October 2021